ANIMAL
GALLERY

THIS BOOK BELONGS TO

....

....

AIM: THIS BOOK HELPS YOU IDENTIFY COLORS , ANIMALS ETC

COLOUR THESE ELEMENTS WITH ANY DESIRED COLOUR

Color the shapes according to the example

WRITE ABOUT YOUR BEST PET

WRITE ABOUT YOUR WORST PET

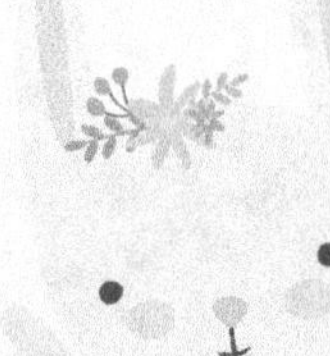

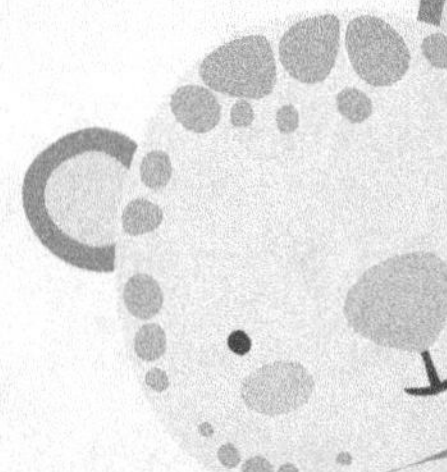

SKETCH YOUR FAVORITE ANIMAL AND COLOR

Draw the animals below and color with desired color

Rabbit

Bear

NAME THE FOLOWING ANIMALS

Name...

WELCOME TO SEA WORLD ANIMALS

Give this hammerhead
shark a grey colour

Name...

Give the shell fish an orange colour

Give the whale a purple color

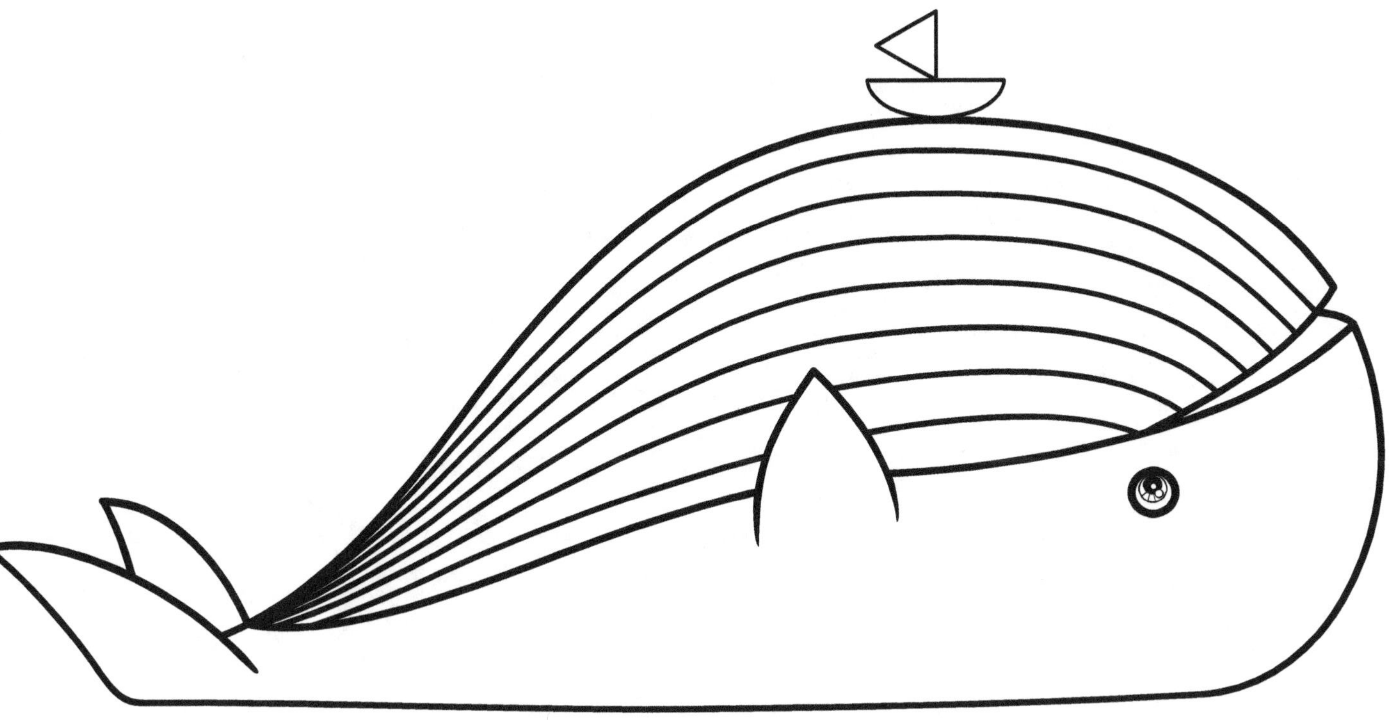

Give this Fish a pink color

Give the crab below a brown colour

Give the shark below any colour of your choice.

colour the giant clam grey

COLOUR THE SEA HORSE WITH DESIIRED COLOUR

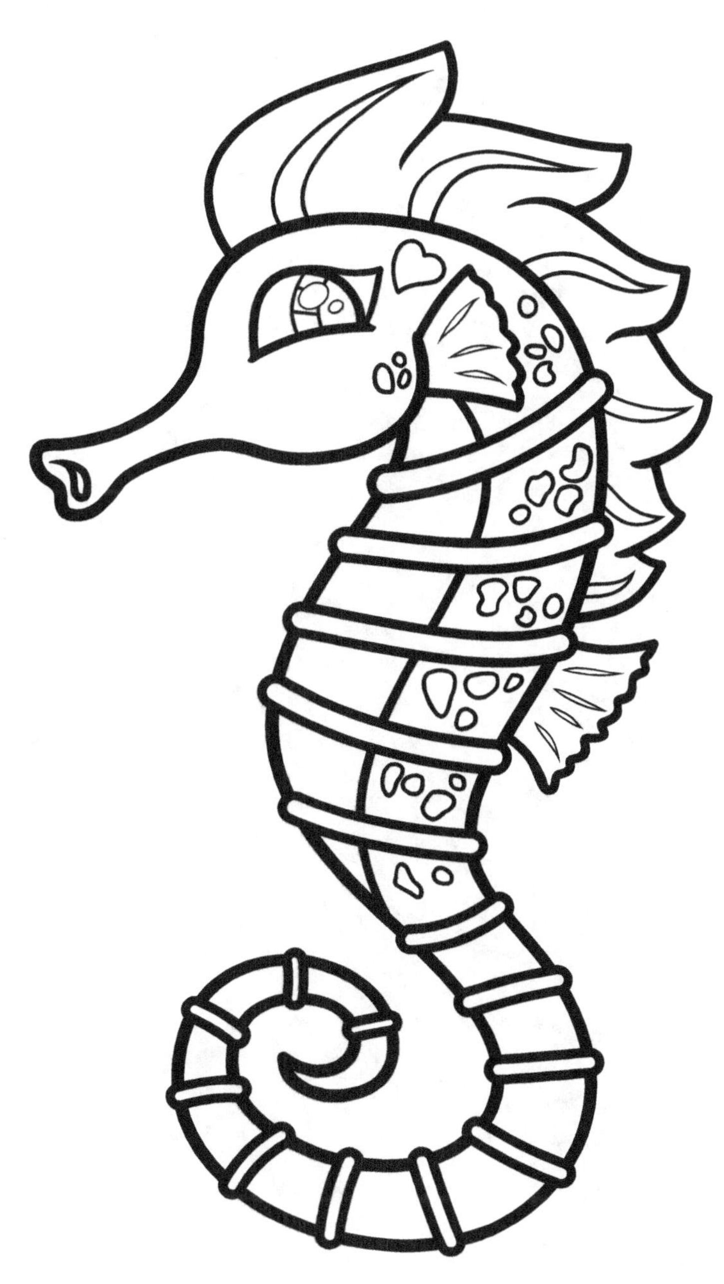

colour the cat fish blue

FROM PAGE 31-52 COLOR THE ANIIMALS WITH ANY DESIRED COLOR AND WRITE OUT THEIR NAMES BELOW

....

···

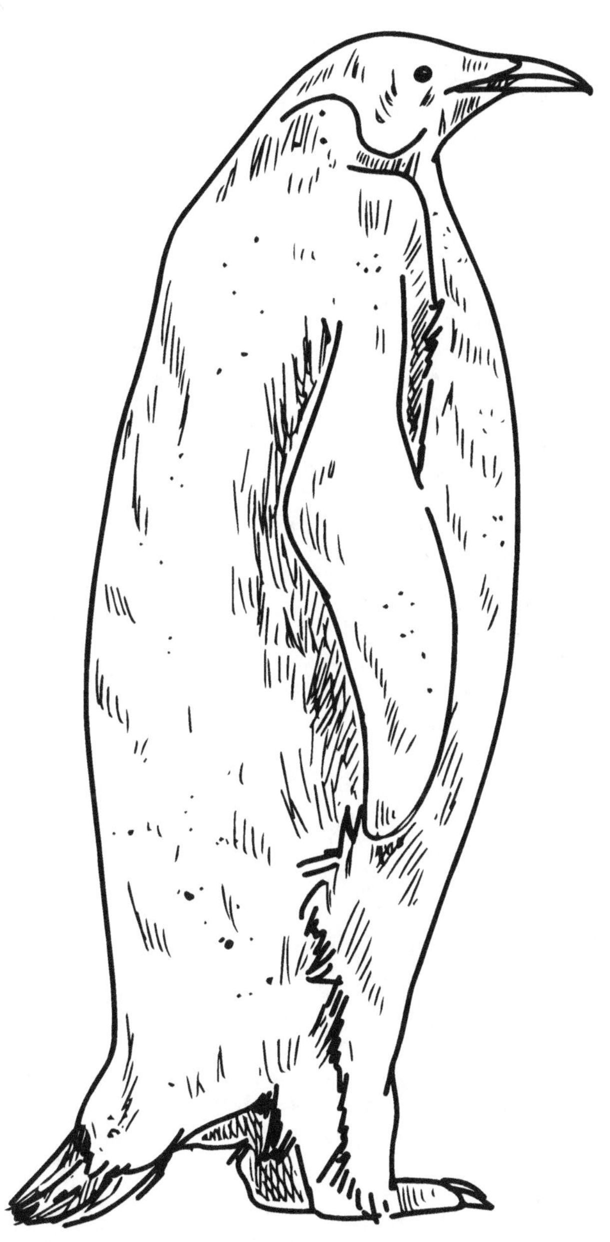

Name...

....

Name..

Flamingo Color by Number

Use the key at the bottom of the page to color the picture.

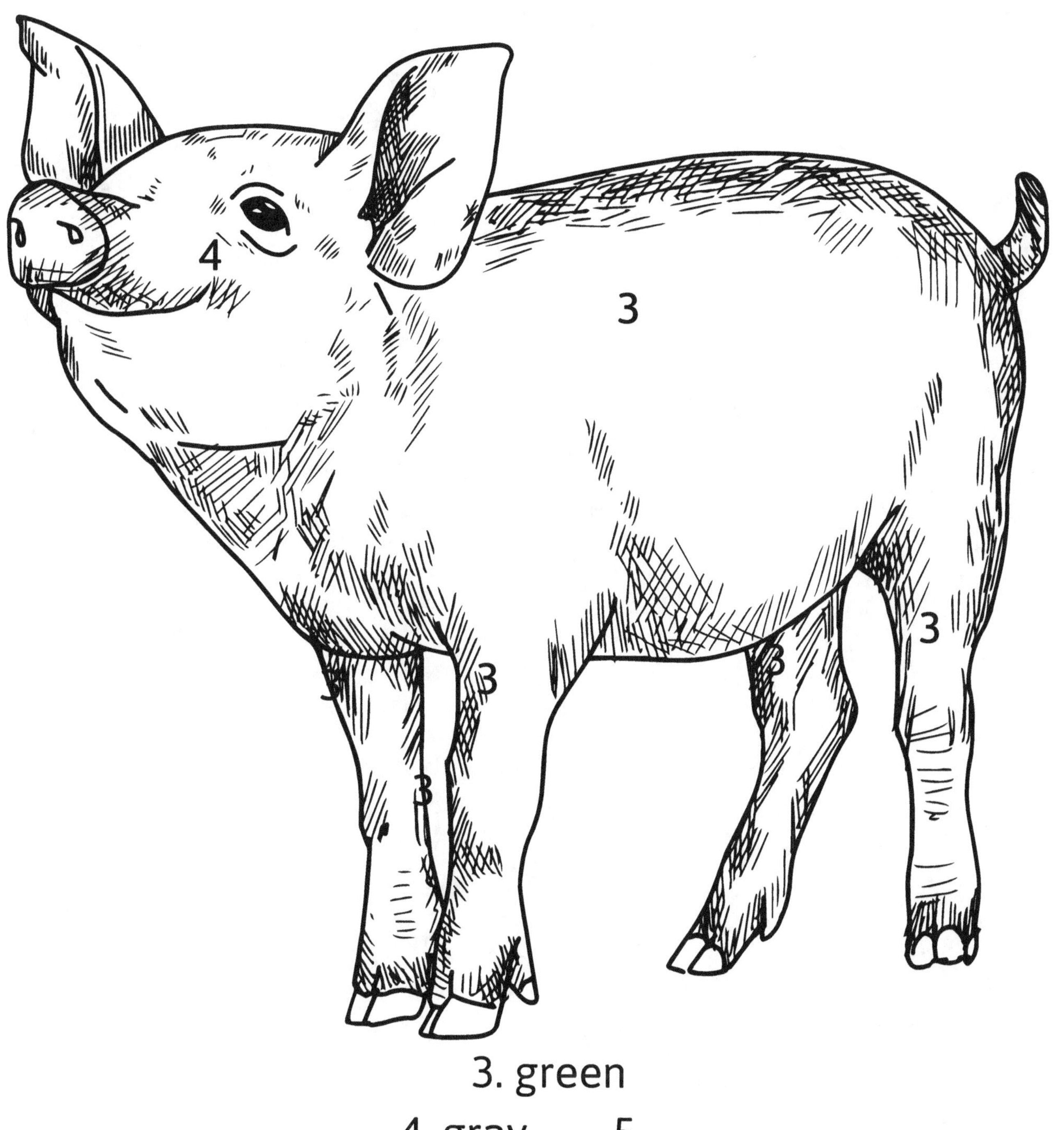

3. green
4. gray   5.

Color by Number - Christmas

Use the key at the bottom of the page to color the picture.

1. gray   2. black   3. white

FARM ANIMALS

connect the mother animals to their babies.

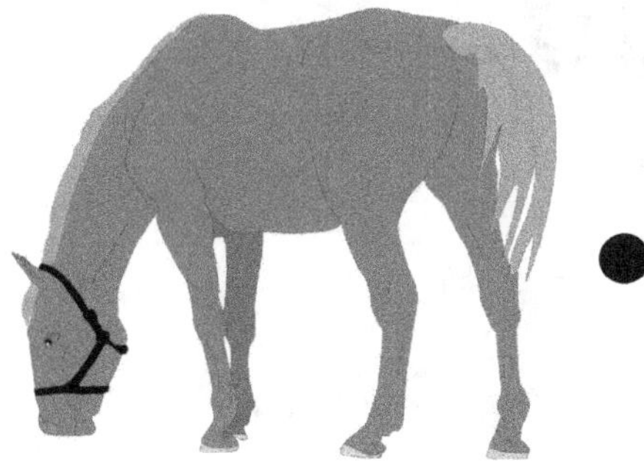

THE FARM

circle all the animals that can be found in the wild.

Identify the animal below and write out the name

....

Identify the animal below and write out the name

....

WORLD WILDLIFE DAY!

Identify the animal below and write out the name

Identify the animal below and write out the name

Identify the animal below and write out the name

···

Identify the animal below and write out the name

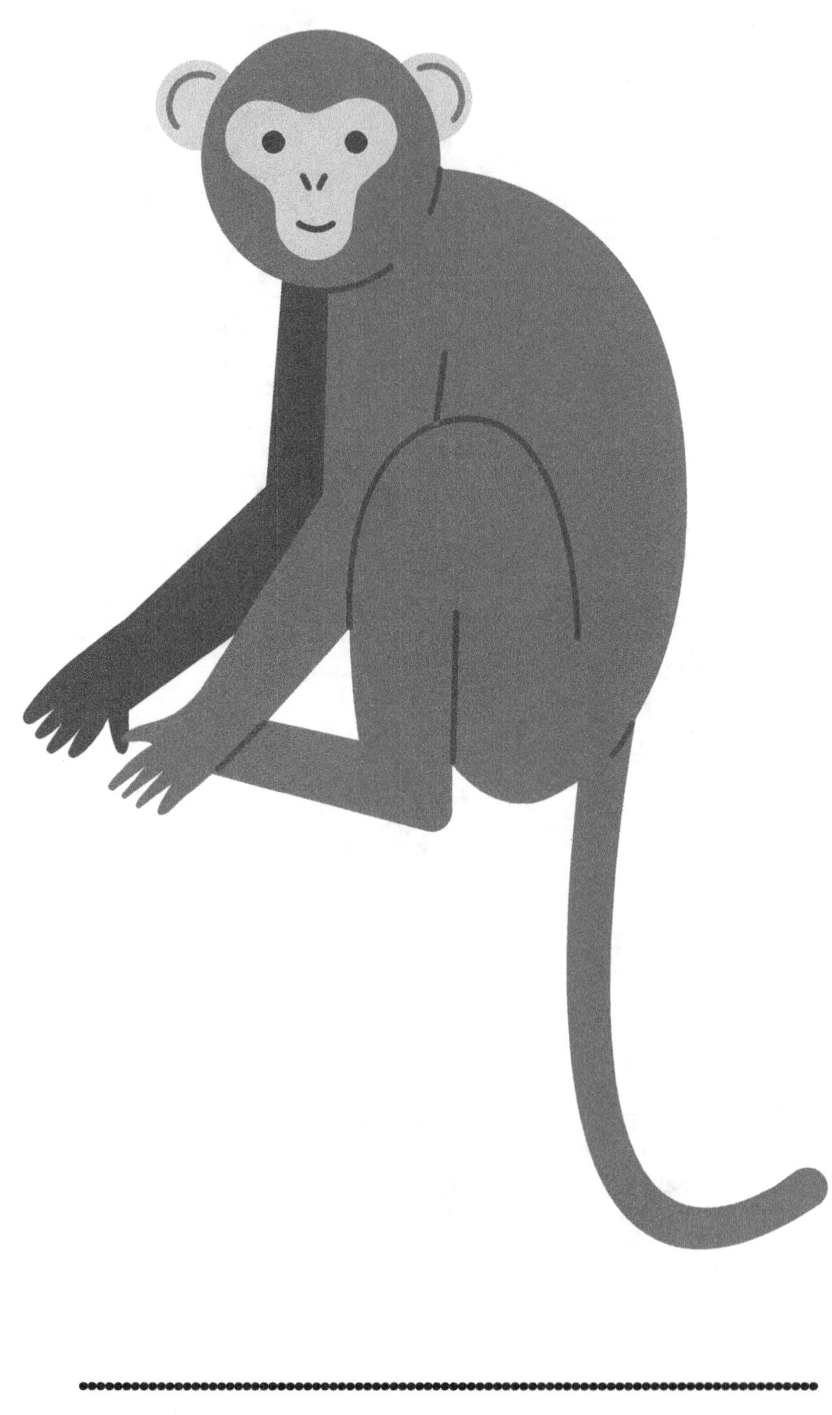

Identify the animal below and write out the name

....

Identify the animal below and write out the name

Identify the animal below and write out the name

....

Identify the animal below and write out the name

ANSWERS

31- cat

33-sheep

35-dog

37-Horse

39-wolf

41-Elephant

43-Crocodile

45-penguine

47-Hen

49-Tortise

51-Giraffe

53-Squirrel

55-butterfly

63- duck

64-Hen

65-Tiger

66-zebra

67-Giraffe

68-Monkey
69-Lion
70-Leopard
71-Crocodile
72-Zebra

THANK
YOU

www.ingramcontent.com/pod-product-compliance
Lightning Source LLC
Chambersburg PA
CBHW081509250726
48662CB00021B/3029